by Joanna Cole

Plants in Winter

Illustrated by Kazue Mizumura

THOMAS Y. CROWELL COMPANY   NEW YORK

Do you like to go to the Botanical Garden? I go there all the time. There I see trees and flowers and lots of greenhouses.

A friend of mine works there. She is a scientist who studies about plants. Her name is Dr. Owen.

One day in winter I went to the Botanical
Garden. Inside the greenhouse it was like summer.
The air was warm and steamy. The jungle plants
were green and growing.

I looked outside. I could not see any green plants. All I could see was snow and the bare branches of trees.

"The plants are all dead in the winter," I said. "They may look dead," said Dr. Owen, "but they are not."

I thought I knew better. I showed Dr. Owen a tree. All its green leaves were gone. Only branches were left. It looked dead.

But Dr. Owen told me that trees lose their leaves in winter to protect themselves from the freezing weather.

"How can losing its leaves protect a tree?" I asked.

Dr. Owen said it would be dangerous for some trees if they had leaves in winter. She told me why.

A tree needs water. It needs to keep water in the cells in its trunk and branches. Without this water, the tree would die.

The leaves need water, too. They use it to make food for the tree. But there are many pores, or openings, in the leaves. A lot of water evaporates into the air through the pores. In the summer the tree can get more water. The roots are always bringing up water from the ground.

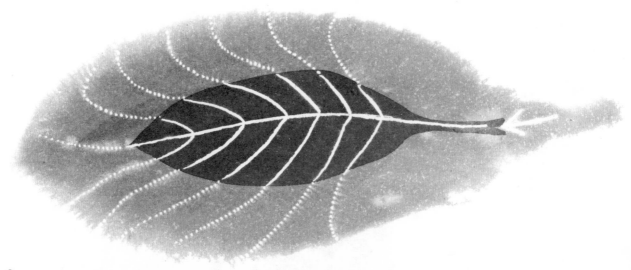

When winter comes, the ground is cold. When it gets too cold, the roots cannot take in water. If a tree had leaves then, all its water would evaporate and it could not get more. The tree would die from lack of water.

That is why a tree must lose its leaves in the fall. It goes into a resting period for the winter.

Dr. Owen showed me that the tree was still
alive. There were hard little buds on all its
branches. When winter was over, the buds would
open into new leaves.

That was a very good thing to know. I was glad
I understood about trees in winter. But then I
thought of something else. I asked Dr. Owen,
"What about pine trees? They stay green all
winter. Why don't they shed their leaves in the
fall too?"

Dr. Owen did not answer my question right
away. First she said, "Look at a pine needle."

It is green. It is a leaf. But it is a special kind of leaf. It is a water-saving leaf. It is small. Not as much water can evaporate from a small leaf as from a big one. The pine needle has a tough, waxy coat that keeps the water in. That is why a pine tree can keep its leaves all winter.

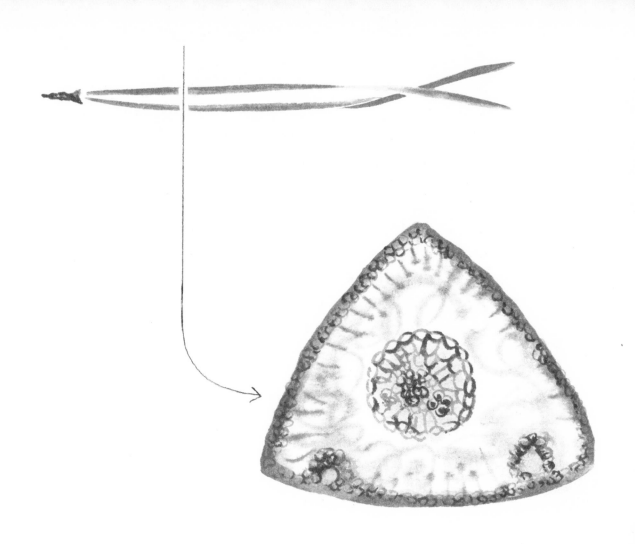

We looked at all the evergreen plants we could find. Dr. Owen was right. Most of them had small leaves. And all the leaves had tough, thick coats.

Now I knew about two kinds of plants. I knew about leafy trees and about evergreens. I knew how those plants lived through the cold winter.

Spruce

Holly

Azalea

15

Crocus

Clover

But then I thought of something else. I asked about the little plants.

"They don't have woody trunks. They don't have water-saving leaves. They die in the winter and come up again in the spring by magic."

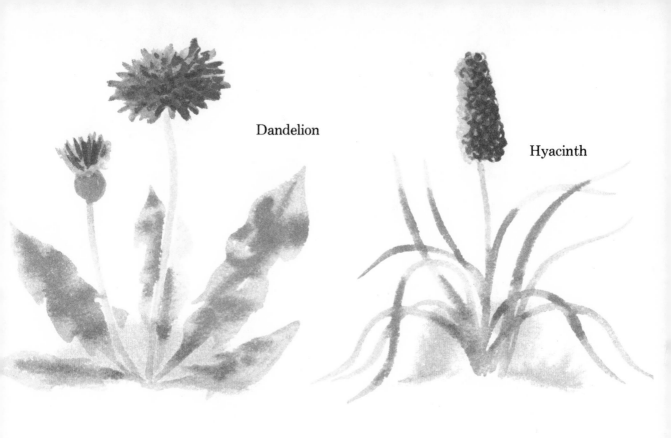

Dandelion

Hyacinth

Dr. Owen laughed. "It is not magic," she said. "They don't die. They protect themselves during the winter too."

Some have a thick stem under the ground. When winter comes, the green plant is killed. But its underground stem is still alive.

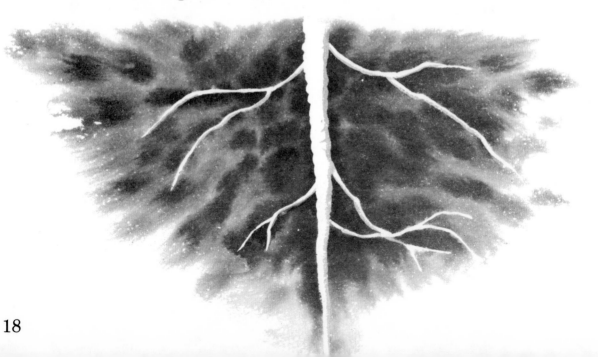

It stays buried all winter, safe under the earth,
away from the cold air. In the spring a new plant
grows from the underground stem.

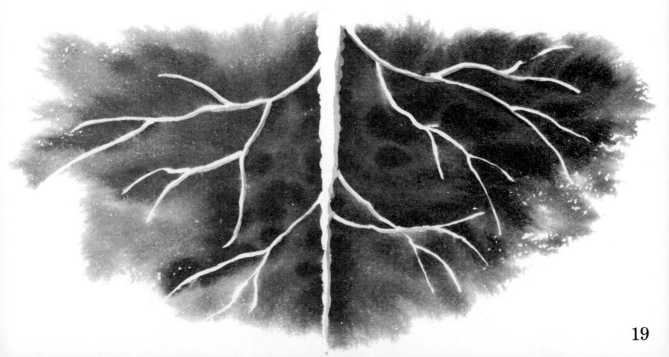

Daffodils, tulips, irises, potato plants—all these have underground stems. We went to the place where the tulips bloom in the spring. We dug into the hard ground. There was an underground stem. We call it a tulip bulb. It looked dead. But it was not.

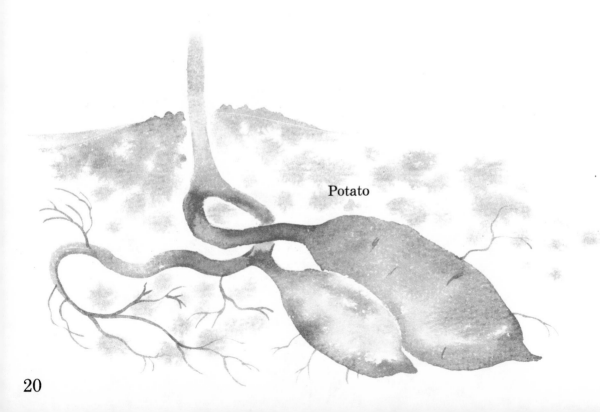

Potato

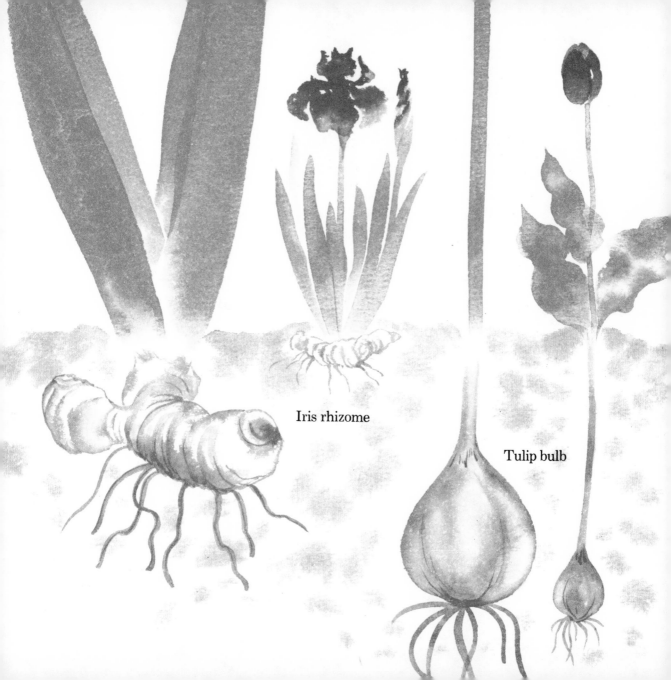

Iris rhizome

Tulip bulb

Other plants have shoots and buds hidden in the top layer of soil. Grass plants are like this. The shoots get shelter under the soil and come up green in the spring. That is why you do not have to plant a new lawn every year.

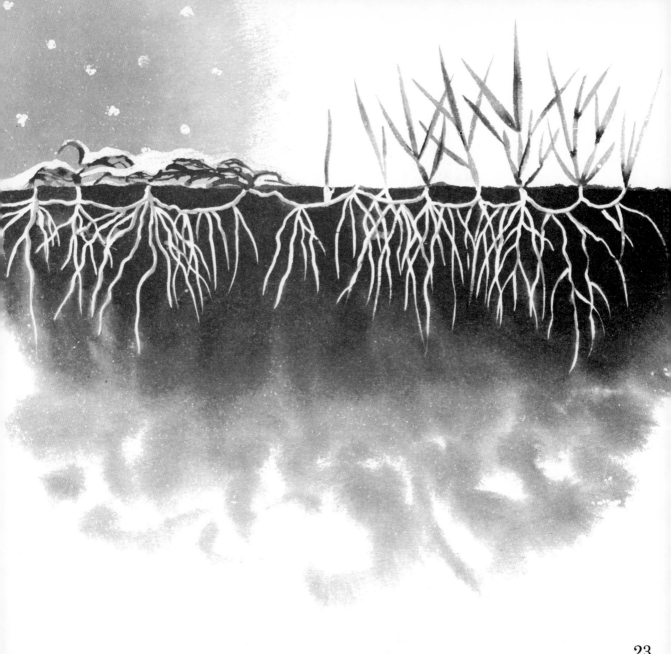

23

There are other plants that do not have bulbs or shoots underground. A morning glory vine is killed by the cold. The plant dies, but it leaves seeds behind. The seeds are alive. They lie in the ground all winter. In the spring new plants grow from the seeds.

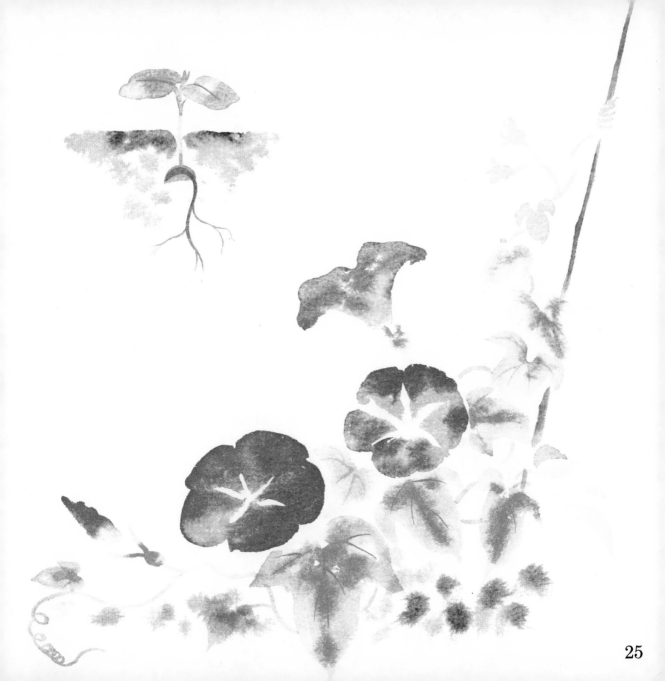

Now I thought I knew all about plants in winter. I knew about leafy trees and evergreens. I knew about plants with underground bulbs and shoots. And I knew about plants that grow from seeds.

But one day I found a flower growing in the snow. It had soft green leaves and a stem and white petals. I ran to get Dr. Owen.

"It is a snowdrop," she said. "It grows from a bulb, like a tulip, but it blooms in the winter."

The snowdrop was very beautiful. We just looked at it for a while.

"How can it grow in the winter?" I asked.

Dr. Owen thought for a minute. Then she said, "No one knows *exactly* how a snowdrop can grow in the snow. Maybe you will find out some day."

That was a very good answer. When I become a plant scientist, I am going to find out about the snowdrop. Because no one knows *all* about plants in winter—yet.

ABOUT THE AUTHOR

Born in Newark, New Jersey, Joanna Cole grew up in East Orange. After attending the University of Massachusetts and Indiana University, she was graduated from the College of the City of New York with a B.A. in psychology. Later she took courses in education at New York University, and worked as a library-teacher in a Brooklyn elementary school. Now she lives in New York City with her husband and devotes a good deal of her time to writing children's books.

ABOUT THE ARTIST

Kazue Mizumura has long been interested in the world of nature, and this concern is evident in all her books. Miss Mizumura is both author and illustrator of several books for children, and the illustrator of many more. She was born in Kamakura, Japan, and now lives in Stamford, Connecticut. She studied at the Women's Art Institute in Tokyo, as well as at Pratt Institute in Brooklyn, New York. Her busy life includes the making of ceramics and jewelry, for she believes firmly in the importance of handicrafts.